MW01036466

TURNING COMMITTEES INTO COMMUNITIES

by Roberta Hestenes

NAVPRESS
A MINISTRY OF THE NAVIGATORS
P.O. BOX 35001, COLORADO SPRINGS, COLORADO 80935

OUR GUARANTEE TO YOU

We believe so strongly in the message of our books that we are making this quality guarantee to you. If for any reason you are disappointed with the content of this book, return the title page to us with your name and address and we will refund to you the list price of the book. To help us serve you better, please briefly describe why you were disappointed. Mail your refund request to: NavPress, P.O. Box 35002, Colorado Springs, CO 80935.

The Navigators is an international Christian organization. Our mission is to reach, disciple, and equip people to know Christ and to make Him known through successive generations. We envision multitudes of diverse people in the United States and every other nation who have a passionate love for Christ, live a lifestyle of sharing Christ's love, and multiply spiritual laborers among those without Christ.

NavPress is the publishing ministry of The Navigators. NavPress publications help believers learn biblical truth and apply what they learn to their lives and ministries. Our mission is to stimulate spiritual formation among our readers.

ISBN 08910-93028

Unless otherwise identified, all Scripture quotations in this publication are taken from the *Holy Bible: New International Version®* (NIV®). Copyright © 1973, 1978, 1984 by International Bible Society. Used by permission of Zondervan Bible Publishers.

Printed in the United States of America

10 11 12 13 14 15 / 10 09 08 07 06 05

FOR A FREE CATALOG OF
NAVPRESS BOOKS & BIBLE STUDIES,
CALL 1-800-366-7788 (USA)
OR 1-416-839-4769 (CANADA)

TURNING COMMITTEES INTO COMMUNITIES

❖

A WORD OF EXPLANATION

The concepts in *Turning Committees into Communities* origi-
nated in a course I taught for many years at Fuller Theologi-
cal Seminary called "Building Christian Community Through
Small Groups." In that course I brought together my experience
as a staff member and minister in three different churches over
twenty years with the experiences and insights of more than a
thousand pastors and lay leaders serving churches throughout
North America.

During recent years there has been an exciting explosion of
interest in the intentional formation of Christian small groups to
fulfill important purposes in churches—including evangelism
and outreach, Christian learning and growth, support in coping
with difficult personal or societal issues, and nurturing relationships. Small groups typically bring three to twelve people
together on a weekly or biweekly basis in an interactive for-
mat, which may include discussion of Scripture or a book;
sharing personal interests, needs, and concerns; conversation
and planning related to areas of service in the church, family,
community, or workplace; and time for prayer or worship.
Churches that establish strong programs for these kinds of
small groups often grow significantly.

However, new small-group programs often overlook one

important type of small group that is already present in almost all congregations. This small group is called a *committee.* Unfortunately, committees are seldom seen as communities of caring people who build each other up as they accomplish significant work. Helping church committees to become more authentic examples of caring Christian communities while serving is the purpose of this brief essay. It suggests a few principles to help transform traditional church committees into more caring communities. I hope you find it helpful.

LOOKING AT THE CHURCH

How do you see the church? From outside, people often see the church as centered in a building and represented by a pastor, priest, or minister. Those within the church understand that the church is made up of people who share a common faith which draws them together in worship and service.

Those who become active in the leadership of a congregation need to look more carefully at the patterns and practices of church life in order to discover signs of vitality or decay, growth or decline, response or resistance. This is particularly true in churches that have decided to begin significant small-group programs. Unexamined presuppositions or assumptions can hide the roots of conflict and confusion even as the church is experiencing renewal and growth in its small-group programs.

It is not uncommon for people in churches (larger churches particularly) to have at least two different ways of seeing the congregation. These two perspectives are seldom examined or discussed, yet they can powerfully shape the ways people participate in and plan church life. One way is to see the congregation *institutionally,* and the other is to see it *relationally.*

Institutional: The perspective that looks at a congregation institutionally tends to look at the formal power and organization structure of the church. Issues of power and authority surface quickly. Who is in charge of what? What are the key decisions in this church, and who makes them? This view immediately considers the governing board, vestry or council, the pastor or pastors and staff, the committees reporting to the board, and the people who are active in the programs.

4

These two key questions are asked about people: "Can we get them involved in helping the program?" and "Are enough people coming to the program?" The task is to set up and run the program and get people into it. So, whether we label it or not, when we tend to think of programs and the hierarchy of who's responsible for their success, we are thinking of a church *institutionally*.

Relational: By contrast, another way of viewing a congregation is to look at the relationships and interpersonal connections that exist in the church. The perspective that looks at a congregation relationally asks, "What is the level and depth of personal relationships in this church?" "Where are the networks in this church? Who regularly talks to or is connected to whom?" "Do people feel a sense of belonging and closeness?" "Do our members and visitors care about each other and feel cared for?" A primary task from this perspective is to help people move from individualism and isolation to a sense of belonging within a caring community, which nourishes and supports participants in the journey of faith and life.

The relational perspective tends to focus on the various groupings of people in the congregation, such as the couples' fellowships, the missionary prayer groups, the Sunday school classes that have been together for years, the singles' groups, the women's association "circles," the small Bible study or covenant groups. Informal small groups that meet in homes or away from the church building are just as important as groups that meet at the church building. The church is seen as being made up of various groups of people who come together regularly in a large group for worship but form smaller, more intimate communities or "cells" for many other purposes, including study, communication, service, and prayer.

From this relational perspective, the "formal" groups like the board or committees are simply one kind of grouping among many. However, as the number of "informal" small groups grows in a church with a strong small-group emphasis, all these different groups appear equally significant as different ways in which Christian people come together. This relational perspective—that a board or committee is just one type of group among many—is quite different from the view of those with a more traditional, institutional orientation.

5

Conflicting Goals, Distorted People

While both perspectives—institutional and relational—have validity, they do differ. This can cause misunderstandings and problems. The differences can be especially important for the new pastor or lay leader who seeks to lead the church to become more relational than it has been in the past.

The major difficulty occurs when a new leader with relational, community-building eyes unwisely develops relational programs and emphases to the neglect of people who are more programmatically or institutionally oriented. Doing this risks ending up with *two congregations with contradictory goals.* This emphasis may inadvertently develop a lot of small-group participants who prize positive, caring relationships but show very little interest in meeting institutional needs or goals.

The institutional people, on the other hand, may feel overworked and uncared for. These people are sometimes highly committed to institutional goals and may consider the relational people to be too self-centered for much involvement beyond group activities. They may become critical of "selfish" people who want the church to be there for them but do not want to take up the tasks of institutional and program maintenance. They may resent small-group members who do not attend Wednesday or Sunday evening services or who do not want to handle the stewardship campaign in their small-group meetings. Institutional people may oppose starting more small groups, saying, "We need workers in the church school and people to make follow-up calls to visitors. Recruiting is a problem. Some work needs to get done in this church. If people spend all their time in groups, nobody is available to work."

As I have examined these differing ways of seeing congregations—particularly in larger churches—I have discovered that often quite different kinds of people exhibit the two perspectives. With the growing involvement of the baby-boomer generation in the church, differences between generations are evident—differences not only of age but also of priorities and values. Often the institutional group is older and the relational group is younger. I would draw that dividing line around fifty to fifty-five years old now.

Many congregations in the United States are aging, so that people in their late fifties, sixties, and seventies may fill almost all the formal leadership positions in the church. These institutionally oriented people focus on duty, responsibility, and obligation. Shaped by the experience of the Great Depression and World Wars I and II, they often respond to appeals based on denominational and congregational loyalty, or the needs of the church. They can be recruited to fill church positions in which they have little personal interest because "somebody needs to do it." The language of duty and loyalty means a great deal to them.

On the other hand, the people in the relational networks are often very different. Shaped more by the sixties and the Vietnam era, they may be oriented less to the concept of duty and responsibility than to the need for meaning, purpose, and fulfillment. They will use language like "finding and using my gifts" and "becoming what God meant me to be." It is not that they are less virtuous or giving than the older group. Both groups share many things in common, most particularly their common faith. Still, they have experienced life differently and often respond to it in somewhat different ways. The labels of loyalty and duty are simply not powerful motivators for the more relationally oriented. They are not marching to that drum. They will become involved deeply with the life of the church but not always in the same ways that their parents did and do.

Without necessarily being aware of it, people are motivated by their answers to these questions: "What is meaningful for me? What gives significance and purpose to my life?" For people on the institutional side, the institution often meets their need for significance through the opportunity to exercise authority and influence in the formal structures and programs of the church. Institutional leaders may find significance in being decision makers and opinion setters.

On the other hand, relational people tend to feel that significance comes not primarily through the opportunity to exercise formal power, but through meaningful relationships that help hold individuals and families together—experiencing love, building community, finding and maintaining closeness and caring, making sense out of life, making a difference directly in the lives of a small group of people. So they often do not see involvement in the formal structures and programs of the church as essential for them.

Now, if these two groups coexist within one congregation,

and the church is growing, this can be a dangerous and unstable situation. In the extreme, it is possible to create spiritual monsters: people who are grossly distorted and unbalanced in their Christian beliefs and behavior rather than moving toward wholeness and unity in Christ.

On the relational side, people can have all kinds of good feelings but very little interest in service or ministry. Peter Wagner has warned of the dangers of "*koinonitis*": a feel-good kind of small group, so inwardly preoccupied they never reach out to the lost or needy.

Whereas on the institutional side, people may become so tired over the years, so burned-out and disillusioned, they begin to damage others in the church with their cynicism and authoritarianism. This happens in part because they have given out much but have received little by way of care or nurture. Feeling used and not properly appreciated, they may seek ever tighter control even when change and renewal are needed. A finance chairman, church school superintendent, or choir member who works hard to help the church function year after year—seldom receiving much appreciation or praise—may become negative, cross, and controlling.

This, of course, represents the extreme. Most people are a long way from such behaviors on either the relational or institutional side. Yet, consider this summary of some of the possible differences:

Institutional	Relational
Focus on hierarchy	Focus on network of relationships
Task: run programs	Task: help people feel cared for
See structures, numbers	See connections among people
Over fifty years old	Under fifty years old
Duty, loyalty	Self-fulfillment, belonging
Significance from influence	Significance from relationships
Danger: overworked, uncared for, controlling	Danger: self-centered, selfish, uncommitted

◆ ◆ ◆

The challenge on both sides of this continuum—and for a pastor or lay leaders working with both types—is to draw relational people into mission and institutional people into situations where they are cared for.

DRAWING RELATIONAL PEOPLE INTO MISSION

I have found it to be true (contrary to what some small-group materials say) that relationally oriented people organized in Christian small groups seldom "spontaneously" erupt into mission or serious Christian service. It doesn't happen that they meet for weeks having a great time of fellowship, learning to know and love each other, and then, all of a sudden, look at each other and say, "Now, how should we be servants of Jesus Christ and give ourselves away? What hard thing should we do?" That happens sometimes, but it is not the normal pattern if groups have been started with no mention of service.

If, from the very beginning of the group's life together, the leader has not built in the importance of Christian ministry as one desirable purpose, it is difficult to add it later. Covenant groups should ordinarily begin with four key elements: interactive learning, interpersonal sharing, a willingness to become involved in caring and serving, and learning to worship and pray together. From these foundations, wholeness can grow.

The idea of ministry as one of the group's goals doesn't have to be there in a full-blown way at the beginning. But when leaders are trained, the commitment to finding ways of service or ministry should be included in the first definitions of good small groups. When talking about covenants and contracts (shared understandings about the group's goals and the means the group will use to reach the goals), leaders need to be trained to point their groups toward ministry.

There are many ways to explore ministry possibilities. One of the most common is to speak of discipleship or following Christ by caring for others as one goal of the group. (For further help see *Using the Bible in Groups,* Hestenes, Westminster Press.) With a discipleship focus, the desire for obedience to Jesus Christ is explicit in the heart of the group members' covenant with each other. Then everyone will understand that ministry needs to be part of what the group is about.

It is quite difficult (I'm almost willing to say impossible) to take a relational network of people, meeting together in a small-group structure, and impose on them institutional tasks and commitments from outside the group. Institutional types often want to do this. From a duty/loyalty point of view, it seems reasonable. But imposing tasks doesn't work, because it is extraneous rather than arising from within the group's own internal process of setting goals and priorities.

Small groups take on a life of their own as people begin to feel a sense of belonging and ownership. This is normal. Groups function personally rather than impersonally. Once a small group has formed, it begins to build trust and cohesion among its members as a result of its interactions over time. Suggestions from outside are often resisted. When suggestions for change arise from inside the group, from one or more of the members, they are more likely to be considered seriously and even adopted.

Studies of group process show over and over that unless people are seriously involved in helping to set the goals of their group, they are only slightly (if at all) motivated to reach those goals. People commit most to what they themselves have chosen. In particular, relational people won't accept that God wants them to fulfill the institution's agenda just because the institution says so. They seldom recognize the institution as God's authorized spokesman, and they feel little sense of duty toward institutions as such. Whether right or wrong, groups made up of relational people resist outside pressure.

The leadership of one church in which I worked would make a list of service projects, then send that list to all the small groups. They would ask each small group to adopt a service project, expecting in this way to divide up the needs of the church and get everyone involved in meeting them. This strategy didn't work because the thinking behind it was programmatic instead of relational or organic. The feeling was that people "ought to" support the programs.

Another time, the missions chairman asked the small-group pastor to send a memo to all the small groups, instructing them to cancel their group meetings for a certain week to attend a missions program and then to adopt a missionary in each group. The goal was to get the missions giving carried out. If the pastor had done that, the result would have been intense hostility to the missions program by many of the small-group members. It would have been exactly counterproductive.

When things are imposed on a group, the demand comes as an attack on the group's commitments and values. The group then coheres against the outside influence. Group leaders need to be trained to know how to raise issues of service and program involvement inside the structure of the group in such a way that the members understand and adopt the goals as their own. Orders seldom work. Good discussions led by group leaders and members are more likely to succeed.

I'm not saying that people ought to respond this way. I'm just telling you that they often do. So if you want small groups to adopt missions and ministries of whatever type, they have to covenant and commit to do that. In your leadership training group, in your training conference, in your workshops, you should help leaders to introduce the idea of "What kind of ministry would we like to adopt as a small group?" The group members need to be convinced first that mission is part of being a disciple, and second, that one particular task is for them.

Make it a covenant question. In the first covenant discussion or "contract" of a new group, ministry may play a smaller role than the building of relationships. But each time the group recontracts (at least quarterly), the subject should come up again. In that setting, it is possible to provide alternatives that people can consider and decide about. Those alternatives may even be ideas from institutional people, but the group members have the freedom to weigh and decide for themselves.

When a mission is imposed on people, they will do it in the most token of fashions; most of the time, they won't do it at all. But if you build mission into the contracting process and provide some creative possibilities, people are more likely to respond.

When you take this approach, you will soon find something else happening. After a group has been together awhile, concerns will begin to arise within that small group. You could fan that spark or ember into the flame of mission. People may be praying about a particular concern. Given encouragement to follow their ideas, they can take that concern and do something with it.

In fact, God will have more missions for your church than you ever dreamed of if those beginning embryonic desires, concerns, and needs are brought to fulfillment in a mission group structure. The key to bringing this about is for the institutional leaders, especially the paid staff and the trained small-group leaders, to encourage people to carry their concerns into mission. They need to do this both vocally and in practical ways, by granting people the authority to plan and act and encouraging all kinds of lay ministry. (A helpful book is Frank Tillapaugh's *Unleashing the Church*.)

So, the challenge is to build mission in from the beginning of your small-group program. Work into your training structures how to covenant for ministry as a group, and then encourage groups to explore regularly what it means that we are called to be servants of Christ. In this way you give people on the relational side the freedom to wrestle through "In what particular way am I alone and are we together going to fulfill that call?"

To summarize:

◆ Build mission into training structures.
◆ Build mission into the contracting discussions.
◆ Provide possibilities, but let the group choose.
◆ Fan into flame group members' ideas.
◆ Support and encourage lay ministry in all ways possible.

COMMITTEES INTO COMMUNITIES

Now I want to focus on the other side: how to help overworked, under-loved institutional people who live much of their church life in committees and on boards.

Years ago, I was concerned that the small groups I had started were not ministry-centered because I had not worked ministry in from the beginning. I realized that I needed to change the way I handled these small groups. But I also realized that God has given the church a group of people who are already task-centered. They are the kind of people who see a need, commit themselves to it, and work hard to meet it. While we need to encourage relational people into mission, it is just as important to encourage the institutional people who were already in the trenches. These people are often found serving on church committees.

It is crucial not to devalue these people's commitments and their willingness to work for the church. If somebody doesn't do this work, think of all the needs in the church and in the world that are not going to be met! Rather than devaluing or ignoring them, we need to stop taking them for granted. Our challenge is to help the people who are functioning institutionally to experience genuine Christian community in the midst of their task. In that way, while they are in those institutional structures, they will be cared for, supported, and nurtured. In other words, we need to quit using them and start building them—encouraging and supporting them in what they are doing.

At the heart of this task is the issue of committees, because institutionally, we usually don't function as small caring groups; we function as committees. So as a central issue, you have to wrestle through how to help the committees and the boards in the church begin to function more clearly as caring Christian communities involved in service.

Is it possible? Yes. Is it difficult? In some situations, it is extremely difficult. Does it have to be done? Yes, it must be done, especially if you are strengthening the small-group emphases in the church. If you do not work with your board and your official committees to build relationships and strengthen community, you may eventually split your church. It may not split physically, but it will be two congregations that are emotionally distanced from each other, misunderstanding and mistrusting each other.

However, if you start with the strengths of each and move them toward wholeness, then you will find that when committees have a relational component, some relational people are willing to serve on them. They are reluctant to sit on traditional committees, but they will be on committees that know how to be communities because that's the way they want to function. So the same thing that brings them into the relational structure of small groups can bring them into the institutional structure. Transformed committees can be a meeting place for both relationally and programmatically oriented church people. Some churches have found it helpful to rename their committees, calling them "ministry teams." This simple change has led to renewed commitments and energy.

My bottom-line assumption is this: Biblically, God has called us to be in some kind of Christian community. Community is the gift of God *and* a human responsibility by God's grace and power. The universal community of faith takes form concretely in local congregations, which are called to share life together in ways that bear witness to the love and mercy of God.

Congregations may organize their lives in many different ways in order to accomplish particular ends. Committees are a basic structure in most North American churches. This is good news and bad news. The good news is that committees can be a satisfying and productive way to involve the church members in the life and work of the church. The bad news is that committees often are structured and operated in a way that ignores one of the central commands of Jesus—that we love one another.

While committees are a fact of church life, many members of committees do not enjoy serving on them. While some people serve with energy and enthusiasm, many see committees as a "necessary evil" or as a time-eating meeting that is as likely to be deadly dull or anger-producing as it is to be productive and satisfying. In one church, almost all the elders reported that they served on committees because they saw it as their duty to do so, but that they looked forward to the day when their terms of office would be up and they wouldn't have to attend meetings anymore. Another group of church officers was asked what was least satisfying about their activity in the church. One man shrugged, "That's easy—committee meetings!"

Often it seems that pastors dislike committee meetings as much as some of their people do. One pastor told me that he entered the ministry because he liked to help people. Now he is frustrated because he spends so much of his time in committee meetings. Committee meetings and helping people are clearly separate activities in his mind. Another pastor tried to arrange for all the committees of his church to meet on the same night, because that way, he said, "I waste only one night a month."

Somehow, in North American churches we have come to believe that it is more important to follow Robert's Rules of Order in our boards and committees than it is to reflect and demonstrate God's love. Following proper procedures is well and good. But if the way we work in committees becomes routine, impersonal, and uncaring, then serving on a church committee may actually be dangerous for the spiritual health of its members. Instead, church committees need to be caring Christian communities.

This fact presents a major challenge for traditional task-oriented church committees: They must learn new ways of encouraging and supporting each other as they work together. Church committees that learn to function as genuine centers for caring and service can be instruments of renewal and growth in the life of the congregation.

When we function as a committee, we are not excused from God's demands that we love one another. We must come together as whole persons—heart and head, body and spirit. Every time we come together, we bring our whole selves to the meeting, not just brains to think and mouths to discuss and argue. Even if we think we bring only our head—our ideas and the ability to sit for two hours—the whole person is really present, and the needs of all the persons present need to be kept in mind as the meeting is planned and conducted.

So, how do you turn a committee into a community? First, to understand where we are going, look at the following chart. It shows the distinctions between a typical church committee and the kind of "mission" community you want to move toward. Notice that, contrary to what institutional people might fear, a mission community has more commitment to both the task and the other group members than most committees do. A community is ultimately more productive and more joyful than a traditional committee.

DISTINCTIONS BETWEEN
COMMITTEES AND COMMUNITIES

Factors	Committees	Mission Communities
1. Level of commitment:		
To task:	Limited and varied.	Serious commitment.
To other persons in group:	Usually low; casual caring.	High with focused energy.
2. Frequency of meeting:	Two or more hours once a month.	As often as necessary to get task done, within agreed on limits.

15

Factors	Committees	Mission Communities
3. Task assignment:	Determined by structure and appointment; tasks are institutionally determined. What do we need to run program?	Gifts determine assignments: "the particular missions making up the total mission of the congregation are determined by the gifts and callings of the members" (Gordon Cosby).
4. Method of assignment:	Assigned by others (e.g., pastor).	Self-chosen with group input.
5. Responsibility for success:	Low—often vote on things for others to accomplish; separation of authority from responsibility.	High—if we don't do it, it won't happen.
6. Involvement of the whole person:	Assumed, but minimally included.	Taken seriously and time provided.
7. Spiritual gifts:	Usually ignored.	Taken into account
8. Spiritual dimensions:	Little care about "inward journey" of members.	Spiritual accountability; care for personal spiritual life.
9. Sense of work as ministry:	A job to be done: "duty." Highest values: efficiency and productivity.	A ministry to be accomplished: "service." Highest values: love and doing the will of God.

◆ ◆ ◆

   With the goal in mind, let me give you several crucial steps in moving from committees to communities.

Deciding Who Serves

The first step is to decide who serves on the committee or board. This process should begin with serious prayer, asking God to give the "laborers" needed for the board or committee. (In the discussion that follows I will speak of these two groups as interchangeable, even through most committees actually serve as subgroupings of the governing council or board.) I begin here because, structurally, this is where the problem begins in many churches and Christian organizations. If you have the wrong kinds of motivations and processes for nominating people, you will get the wrong people on your boards. You will find those people very difficult to change because they have joined the committees for the wrong reasons.

Is nomination to service on the committee done on the basis of getting people involved? "Susan hasn't been involved in anything lately. Let's get her involved by offering her a position on the council." Wrong approach!

Is service on the board given to recognize distinction or position in the community? "We've got a high school principal, a bank president, a community leader—of course they should be elders in our congregation." Wrong again!

Is nomination given in recognition of wealth? "This person is the biggest giver in our church. He ought to be on the board." Or, "This is a very powerful person in our church. We'd better keep her happy by making sure she's on this committee." Both wrong!

If those motivations drive any part of the nomination process, everything else I'm going to say will be really difficult because you'll have the wrong people on the board. This is not to say that people with wealth, title, or influence should never be asked to serve. But those are the wrong reasons for asking. The New Testament passages on church leadership speak of looking for certain gifts and qualities: such as wisdom and administration, a godly reputation, a strong family, a heart for hospitality, a spirit of servanthood—people "full of faith and of the Holy Spirit" (Acts 6:5). These qualities matter more than human wealth and position.

Life and ministry: A place on a committee or an elder or deacon board should be given in response to a person's walk with the Lord and his or her demonstrated ministry. I draw this conclusion from the requirements given in the New Testament passages concerning those who serve. For example, elders are supposed to be apt to teach, according to 1 Timothy 3. How do you know if a person has that gift? Because he or she has demonstrated a teaching ability in some way, either publicly or in one-on-one sessions with other believers. The quality of people's lives, their faith in God, their family life, the spiritual characteristics the people bring, these are things that nominating committees *must* be taught to consider as crucial factors.

Gifts: The typical nominating committee has heard little if anything about the importance and use of spiritual gifts in ministry. Yet people should be asked to serve based on the spiritual gifts God has given them. These gifts are given by God for the common good to build up the church (1 Corinthians 12, Ephesians 4). We need to match a person's gifts with the committee or board function where the gift or ministry is most likely to be exercised. This means we need to learn as much as we can about the candidate.

One pattern would be that no one should be nominated to a position of formal leadership who has not served in some ministry that shows he or she has what it takes to be effective in serving the congregation; no one should be nominated to a committee who isn't actively involved in the ministries of the congregation somewhere. In this way, new leadership is encouraged to emerge out of the church's life. It isn't the first place you bring people in. I think that's biblical.

Recruiting

The next step in moving from committees to communities is to recruit carefully the prospective board members. You don't even get a chance to do this if all the wrong people have been nominated. But let's hope that the right people are being considered for service. Before placing someone's name in nomination it is important to have a "recruiting conversation" to inform the person of the assignment he or she is being asked to consider and to help him or her make a good decision about accepting the assignment.

This is the typical recruiting speech: "Can you help us out? It won't take much time. We really need you. We would appreciate it so much if you would do this." That is the world's worst speech if you want quality in ministry and a commitment to community from your board or committee member. You need something more.

Job descriptions: First, you need clear job descriptions. Specifically, what are you asking this person to do? What ministry needs to be done? How much time will this committee take, and what results are you hoping for? With whom will the person be working? What is needed to get the job done?

Do you know what the average job description—the hidden job description—is for an elder? "Come to as many board meetings as you can manage. Sit through the two-hour meetings and listen to any presentations. Express your own views when appropriate, and then vote." This is a minimal-functional job description. And it is a terrible job description. It is guaranteed to give bad results.

If you want a ministry commitment from someone, you better have a serious conversation with her or him about what you're looking for. If you want prayer from him, that ought to be in his job description. If you want large amounts of time and energy between meetings, you must tell the person ahead of time. If you want certain kinds of results from the ministry, you need to make that plain. If you hope that members of the board will learn to care for each other as they do the work of the board, you will want to make that clear up front.

There is a big difference between sitting in a meeting and getting something accomplished. You need to be clear about what you hope for and expect. Clarity during recruiting helps people make more informed decisions. When they join the team, they enter in more quickly and stay involved longer. Honesty matters. People recruited with low expectations may bring low energy to the tasks that need to be done.

You can see that in order to present a job description to a prospective committee member, you have to pray, strategize, and think the matter through ahead of time. At one church I worked with, we took our Session on a retreat every year. Among other activities, all of the elders wrote job descriptions for what it took to get the ministry done in their particular area of responsibility. Those job descriptions were given to new people being recruited. We told them, "Here is what this ministry involves; here is what it will take to accomplish the work in this area of the church's ministry. This is what we hope you will care about. Are you interested and able to do that?"

Real care: As part of recruiting, you want to express real care for the person. Beware of telling and selling. You need to listen attentively to the other person. I once knew an elder of a key committee who simply didn't function well. It turned out that his job was a mess, his family was a mess, his life was a mess. He was a good and decent man who happened to be overwhelmed at that time in his life. He should never have been asked to serve, particularly in the time-demanding committee chairmanship to which he was assigned. But he could squeeze out two hours a month, so he had accepted. Nobody had taken the time to ask, "How is life going for you? How's your family? How's your marriage? How's your job right now?"

If a person tells you that it's a high-demand time and he's working nineteen hours a day, you don't need to say, "Will you squeeze this in?" Instead, ask, "Is that going to continue, as you see it, over the next period of time? Could this assignment be worthwhile in your life? Are you able to rearrange some of your priorities?" Then he can determine whether or not this is the best time. If the marriage is in trouble or they are just not seeing much of each other, you'll find out if you ask, "How's your marriage?" If the person responds with a wan smile, "Well, it's great—I think—the last time we had a chance to talk," then you may get a feeling that they're not seeing much of each other.

You need to pay attention to these things, because they will affect the person's performance on the committee *and* because you are demonstrating how a caring community operates. You care for the person. That's a primary message. It's not that you just care to fill a job. It's not just to put a body in a slot.

This is a pastoral conversation. Ask the person, "How are you doing spiritually?" Some church members would faint if this were asked in recruiting interviews. In fact, in one church when they decided to ask prospective elders how they were doing spiritually, one man responded, "It's none of your damn business." Oh, really? His attitude was, "What's that got to do with anything? That stuff is personal and has nothing to do with my becoming an elder or a deacon."

That person should have been immediately removed from consideration. Instead, he was selected to be on the board. The nominating committee was so intimidated that they concluded, "Well, really, we guess we're not supposed to ask each other how we're doing spiritually," and they backed way off. Instead, when a person says, "Well, I don't know that I want to talk about that," it may indicate a serious problem. Elders uninterested in discussing spiritual matters are unlikely to contribute in a positive way as you seek to encourage the development of prayer and caring in the group.

Exploration of possibilities: In every conversation, you have to consider that the timing of service may be "if not now, maybe later." Some of these conversations will not recruit somebody for immediate involvement. My best people have been recruited in conversations in which, as I listened to their concerns, I said to them, "This doesn't sound like it's a good thing for you to do right now. How about if I come back in six months? Or a year?" If you have a long-term commitment to your church and a long-term strategy, then you can do that kind of thing. If you're always putting out fires, then it's difficult.

Then, when the six months or the year is up, you come back. Many times people have gotten those aspects of their lives together and they're ready. They'll make a real, substantial commitment when you give them adequate time to prepare to serve in this new way.

Delayed decision: I follow the philosophy of "Never let somebody answer 'yes' or 'no' on the first conversation." I don't know about you, but many pastors and lay leaders are relatively strong and have some ability to manipulate people. I have learned that people I have pressured or manipulated into jobs do not have a sense of call from God. They have a sense of having said "yes" only out of loyalty to me. I don't want things done out of loyalty to me. I may let them down or disappoint them. I want people to know that God has called them to ministry.

So I present it this way: "Here's what it is going to take. This is why it is important. Here's the work involved. Here are the kinds of commitments we're asking for. Let's pray about it, and I'll give you a call next week." People often give me a preliminary answer, and I say, "Talk to your spouse. Think about it." And every once in a while, they come back and say, "You know, I thought about it, and it's not a good thing to do right now." I make it easy for them to say no, so they don't feel coerced. Most of the time they say yes, but they feel good about the yes because it was thought about and prayed about, and they had a little room to maneuver.

All of these are principles, by the way, that come out of healthy small-group dynamics. Can you see how they do? They give people freedom, room to move around, room to choose, room to buy in. When people do that, they commit in a different and more substantial way. That's why it's worth the time and energy.

Sense of high calling: I try to convey this attitude: "We're not asking you to do a job; we're asking you to consider a ministry." The recruiter needs to express a sense of vision, with enthusiasm for the ministry. There is a difference between a job and a ministry. A ministry is something that I do because I believe God has called me to it, and I am willing then to pay the price of the ministry even if it is challenging and costly. So a key question is, "Is this something God is calling you to do? I know I'm bringing you the request, but is it something God has asked you to do?"

Support: You need to ask, "What help will you need to fulfill the job expectations?" Tell them what help and training is available. Sometimes the standard thing to say is, "We'll give you all the help in the world," and then they never see you again. Instead, listen to what help they think they need, then develop some training accordingly.

I once needed potluck dinner coordinators for groups of new members to get acquainted with long-time members of the church. We had eighteen potluck dinner groups going. The previous coordinators had resigned, and I needed new ones. I started praying about who that should be. It was several months before a certain couple came very strongly to mind. I saw them and said, "Hey, I want to talk to you about something. There is a ministry that I think might be right for you. Could you come to my house? We'll talk about it."

So they came to the house, and we talked. I had to say to them, "Basically, the ministry is that you will be the pastors to a flock of about two hundred people. You will need to organize, encourage, and problem solve in relating to them. There are almost no financial resources available, and I'm able to give

22

you only a limited amount of time because, at the moment, I'm overextended. You will have a support group in the committee that oversees this work. But you're basically going to be working hard and carrying major responsibility. It's going to be tough. There are significant rewards because of the difference you can make in hundreds of lives. God can do a lot through this kind of ministry. But it's going to cost you. Now pray and think about it."

We were discussing these matters back and forth; it wasn't all one long speech. When I got to the end of my speech, they looked at each other and smiled. I said, "Okay, what's that smile about?" It was one of those funny smiles. He explained, "In the car on the way over here, we said, 'If this is another one of those mickey-mouse church jobs, we don't want it.'" They were hungry for something significant to do. As it turned out, they functioned in an outstanding way for over eight years in that form of pastoral ministry. They were gifted and ready. They committed and stayed committed. They didn't just sit in a committee. Using the committee as a base of support, ideas, and planning, they carried out a wonderful ministry.

When we talk people into things, we're constantly having to recruit for the same positions over and over again. When God calls them into ministry through a prayerful, careful recruiting conversation, sometimes people find new meaning and purpose in their lives, and they enjoy a ministry that God is really giving them.

The First Training Experience
It is very important that you set new norms or shared expectations for how you're going to function as a committee or board. The new norms need to be in the recruiting job description. Part of this job description is that you expect to train your new members, and this specific training is part of the requirements for the office. In one former church, we required all the elders to participate in four weeks of training before they joined the board.

In that training experience, you set new norms and build relationships. You use questions to promote sharing, pray conversationally with each other, indicate task definitions, and send a message: "We care for each other as we do the work of ministry. We are committed to each other as well as to the work God has given us to do together. We are interested in each other as persons as well as interested in our particular assignments." Part of the training should be on how to build relationships in your committees by using sharing questions, conversational prayer, and other techniques. Sharing questions are one-sentence questions that give people permission to talk about themselves without requiring inappropriate self-disclosure. The training should also include help in developing significant prayer times.

Common themes to interact on include telling each other about your own journey of faith, talking about hopes and fears, and expressing personal concerns and prayer requests for both the work and each group member. If you rotate elders every three years, as many churches do, and each time train the new elders in how to build community, you will gradually transform the way in which people expect to work together. If every new elder is trained in this new model, you can revitalize your board by the end of the three years because you have trained them in a new pattern.

The Yearly Retreat

If you want committees to function as communities, I strongly recommend that you take each committee on a yearly retreat. It should be at least a Friday night and Saturday. Three days is better if the schedule will permit. Find out what the members are willing to do. If you have never taken the board on a retreat, you may want to begin simply with a one-day experience.

It is best to meet in comfortable surroundings away from your church building. A nearby retreat center or conference grounds may be suitable. A church with good facilities in a neighboring community may be a good place to use. If you have no money available for housing, you can meet in somebody's home on Friday night, going home and returning for a full day on Saturday. You don't have to go away in order to have a positive experience; you just need to schedule an extended period of time with each other in comfortable surroundings. You need time to get to know each other away from your regular routines and responsibilities. Preparing meals together, walking, playing, singing, praying, talking, planning, and resting can all be valuable.

Committee or board meetings of two hours per month

24

allow little time for strengthening relationships among members. You don't have enough time. This also isn't good for extensive problem solving or creative thinking. The typical committee—meeting for two hours—has enough time to work through only the first stage of the problem-solving process: What is the problem? By the time that is thoroughly discussed, it's time to go home! This doesn't leave time to work through solving the problem. If you have a major issue to work on, you need the kinds of relationships and time where you can do it.

I'll give you two examples. The Session at one church goes on a retreat every December. New elders are recruited months before the time of the annual elders' retreat. If some people cannot make the retreat, their absence indicates that God may not be calling them to be on the Session at this time. The retreat is a required part of what it means to be on the Session. This church is usually low-key and somewhat informal but found this requirement of attendance essential to the vitality and health of the board.

When I was at this church, we spent a lot of time at the retreat building relationships, sharing vision, working together in teams, goal-setting, and praying together. Goals were evaluated from the past year and set for the next year with management-by-objectives principles. Everyone learned how to set goals for effective work. They also learned that effective planning could be combined with enjoying each others' company and getting to know each other better as persons with a life outside of church. The group evaluated the last year confident that others wished them well even though they were less than perfect; they set goals for the next year knowing that the others would care about and support them in their efforts. But they also spent time getting to know each other and praying for each other. All the other meetings of the year drew strength from the relationships built on that retreat.

In the adult education committee, we worked to have a retreat each May. We either went away or stayed in a home where we could spend a serious amount of time with each other. We spent at least four hours at different times in relationship-building and prayer together. Then we took a major area of the church's life, and we brainstormed and prayed together about how to tackle it from the standpoint of our committee. A family life ministry might be the subject for one year. Evaluating and developing new small groups might be the subject for another year. Developing a program of spiritual formation was the theme another year. One new area would be considered along with the regular activities of the committee. Setting aside time for retreat gave us enough time to work through the problem and share dreams in a way that helped bring them to fruition. It also taught us that we did not work alone but with brothers and sisters committed to working with us. This gave new energy to our activities.

Remember, when I talked about recruiting new committee members, I mentioned job descriptions. The retreat is a great place to let each member write down his or her job description and ask others for their input. Another exercise I've found invaluable is to have each person answer the questions on the "Clarifying Expectations" worksheet (see page 27). Its purpose is to find out what a person thinks he or she is supposed to do, *and* what he or she thinks others are supposed to do. It's amazing how much resentment, frustration, and confusion you can defuse when Alice learns that Meg had no idea Alice expected her to be doing a certain task in a certain time-frame.

Here is how to use the "Clarifying Expectations" worksheet:

1. Give each person fifteen minutes alone to complete it.
2. Compare answers one question at a time in the group as a whole. Ask people to clarify and keep talking until you are satisfied that everyone understands how everyone else sees his or her answer.
3. Resolve conflicts among different expectations through discussion.
4. Write your conclusions in the training manual for this committee, so that everyone knows what is expected of each person.

You should be able to get through the whole exercise in two hours.

The key to a good retreat is to achieve a balance between relationship building, task work, and relaxation. You need fun time and good food, but you also need good task work and good relationship activities because you're setting new foundations for future patterns of interaction and work.

CLARIFYING EXPECTATIONS:
ROLES AND RESPONSIBILITIES IN COMMITTEE WORK

---

1. What is the purpose of your committee?

2. Within the overall and specific purposes of your committee's responsibility for _____ who is responsible for *what*?

3. List and describe specific tasks and responsibilities for each of the following as you best understand them now.

   a. The committee chairperson:

   b. The members of the committee—collectively and individually:

   c. The pastor or pastors:

   d. Any program or support staff—such as secretaries, maintenance people, etc.:

   e. Interns, volunteers, or other committed persons:

◆ ◆ ◆

Community in Regular Meetings

Having begun some good patterns in the retreat, you need to continue a pattern of personal interaction and prayer in every regular meeting. This doesn't have to take the bulk of your time. You can divide into groups of two or four, and for five to ten minutes, have them talk about one concern they want prayer for. Then allow a time of prayer. You can break into groups of four and give them fifteen minutes to work on something related to the lives of the members and the work of the group.

Sharing questions are your basic tools to promote communication. Remember, sharing questions are one-sentence questions that give people permission to be personal and talk about themselves without violating their dignity or requiring inappropriate self-disclosure. Sharing questions are often used as a "warm-up" and preparation for prayer. Examples include: What is one challenging situation in your life right now? When did you first experience success, and how did it impact you? What do you do on a typical Tuesday? What is your favorite season of the year, and why? What was your most meaningful Christmas (Easter, birthday, etc.)? What do you find energizing and what do you find draining in your church assignment? What is one thing in your personal life and one thing in your church work about which we can pray?

Here is a useful principle if you want to change from an institutional to a more relational church: *The sharing questions should be related to the task of the group.* A sharing question for an evangelism committee, for instance, could be: "When did you come to faith in Christ, and what was most helpful for you in that process?" Task-oriented types aren't too fond of "touchy-feely" sharing questions. So you want to ask them questions that are related somewhat closely to the task at hand. For the worship committee, the question might be: "What's the most important experience of worship that you've ever had, and what made it special?" People communicate, and it's personal, but they're sharing around the task. For the Christian education committee: "What do you remember about being a child in church school? Was it good, bad, or indifferent, and why?" You're sharing, but you're also gathering information that is going to help when you come to decision making. During

Easter planning ask: "What is the significance of Easter for you, personally?"

Another point to keep in mind: Generally, *if you spend time sharing at the beginning of the meeting, the speeches later on will be more brief, and the time of the meeting will not be extended.* In fact, a time of sharing shortens the meeting, because committe and board members often feel a need to register their presence or to make a speech. If they've had a chance to make that speech in a sharing time—either in the whole group or in a smaller subgroup where they've been listened to and prayed for—they very often do not have to work out their need to be heard or their frustrations, anger, hurt, or disappointment by making long speeches on agenda items later in the meeting.

When we first introduced sharing into one large church board, I was told it would never work. Our Session meetings were going past eleven o'clock every time. You almost hated to go because you never knew when you would get home. We had hassles and hassles and more hassles. But we started a time of sharing, and the Session meetings actually dropped in length. The warmth and quality in the meeting improved. We were done before ten o'clock every time. It was just amazing. When people felt cared for, they could participate in a different way.

But there is a proviso that goes with this: *You have to know how to plan a good meeting,* so that when you come to the agenda setting and problem solving, you do them efficiently. This is why management principles are so important. If you run a sloppy meeting and then add time for sharing, people will say, "We don't have time for that." So you have to learn how to run an efficient meeting that focuses on the essential matters. A prepared, written and distributed agenda, indicating the expected length of time needed to handle each item, can help you be more efficient. Begin and end on time. Consider having a fifteen-minute sharing time at the beginning, then distribute the agenda. Plan one or two discussion questions, so everyone can talk. You have to know how to move a discussion through systematic problem solving by regularly summarizing and moving the group to decisions and action. And you have to teach members to do their homework ahead of time, so that everyone is ready when you come to a particular discussion. Otherwise, an institutional, task-oriented group of people will say every time, "The sharing and prayer have to go. We don't have time for that." End each major discussion by asking questions of implementation: e.g., Who will take responsibility for this? When will it be done? Who needs to be informed? When meetings are well-planned and executed, the more personal time is valued and anticipated.

Expanded Committees

If you have only elected elders or deacons or officers of that type on your committees, consider expanding the committees. Put laypeople on alongside the elected elders, if your church rules permit this. Let an elder serve as the chairperson, with laypeople as full members. Then the committee becomes a laboratory for developing future leadership. In churches that have only elders on their committees, new potential leaders have few opportunities to get involved in significant activity. This can be devastating to renewal and growth because laypeople can represent new life and future elders. So if you have three elders on the worship committee, recruit three to nine laypeople to work alongside them as a ministry team in the area of worship. You will have more people power to get tasks done, you will have a team to work with, and you will be cultivating for the future.

Caring Outside the Meeting

Now consider the pastor's or the committee leader's care for the people. I have written previously about an experience I had with an elder whom I asked to go to lunch. After we'd had our lunch, he leaned back and said, "Now, what is it that you want?" I said, "I don't want anything. I just want to hear how you're doing and how things are going. I want us to have a chance to talk." He said, "Oh, come on! I have never been to lunch with pastors when they didn't want something."

We think people can't read us. Do you spend any time with your key leaders in which *they* are the agenda—not the job, not their performance? Do you indicate that you are simply interested in them by listening—not talking about how to solve a problem, not lobbying them to support your position on an issue? Do you ask, not "How is the work going?" but "How are you doing?" Have you expressed affirmation, not just for their performance on the job, but for them as people and what you appreciate about them? Caring, listening, relationship time between meetings makes all the difference in what happens in a meeting.

Caring also includes going to their territory, where they are the ones in control. Do you go to their offices? Do you sit in their homes? Or do you have conversations only on your territory, where you are the power figure? Are you a listening, caring, supportive person? Do you take them seriously?

One of the gifts that we as church leaders can give to board and committee members is our time. Too often in churches, the people who get our best time are those who complain and those who are in great personal difficulty. One national leader often speaks to pastors of the danger of being bound by "the tyranny of the uncommitted." To build strong, healthy leaders for the present and future ministry of our churches, we need to invest significant amounts of time in people who may not demand it or expect it. Yet as we share our lives with them, as Jesus shared His life with the twelve disciples, we become part of the process of discipleship that produces leaders for the future.

If we use our time only instrumentally, people can feel that they are being used. But if we use some of that time more personally, people appreciate and respond to it. They know the difference. Then you won't have the kind of thing that is typical in many churches. I have interviewed hundreds of elders and asked them how they felt about being an elder, and the average response has been, "I'll be so glad when this term of office is over." If you are treating your people right, their response will be, "I will be sorry when this particular form of ministry comes to an end." People ought to leave their terms of office more committed, more encouraged, more supportive than when they started. And if they are not, then we are not working with them in the right ways.

One elder, Hal, who had served for many years on church committees, seldom spoke up in meetings and never said anything about himself. During the first day-long retreat of the committee, time was taken for talking about personal concerns and needs for prayer. Slowly and uncertainly, Hal shared very briefly about his concern for his daughter who was in some difficulty. Then the committee members spent about half an hour in prayer for each other. Finally, toward the end of the prayer time, one group member prayed for Hal and his daughter by name. As we lifted our heads, we saw a brightness come into Hal's face as he wiped away a furtive tear. "I think I just found out what the church is supposed to be: It's a community that cares," he said. In that moment, we all knew we were more than just a committee. We were a community bound together in love, rejoicing with those who rejoice and weeping with those who weep (Romans 12:15). We went on to the rest of our work with joy.

YOU CANNOT FAIL

The last thing I want to say is that you cannot fail in this ministry in the ultimate sense because this is a work that God is doing in His people. There are things we do that are really not in the center of the will of God, and they can be uphill and hard. However, when we build people into communities, we can know that we are working in the flow of the Holy Spirit to build the Church, and that when things are hard, they may be hard because God wants to do something deep, lasting, and significant.

We take our encouragement not from our own skill or techniques. It isn't because we master textbooks or learn techniques or know certain routines. Our basic encouragement for this work is that Jesus has promised that He will build His Church, and He has chosen to use humans—us—as part of that process.

So when I get discouraged with myself or with my people or with the structures or the situations, I come back to home base. Home base is to remember that this church is God's; it's not mine. God cares about building it and wants me to trust His work in me, in the people, and in the situation.

Exercising faith, living in the power of the Holy Spirit, and making ourselves available to Him, without being unduly reliant on our own abilities, gives us the kind of peace that makes forward movement possible. Our churches will never be perfect, but they can be wonderful places of learning and service in which more and more people discover the wonderful adventure of life together in Christian community.